D1593661

Ruffles & Flourishes

Ruffles & Flourishes

A Guide
to Customs
and Courtesies
of the
Military

by
Judy K. Beam

Daring Books
Canton • Ohio

Published by Daring Books
P.O. Box 20050, Canton, Ohio 44701

Library of Congress Cataloging-in-Publication Data

Beam, Judy K., 1942-
   Ruffles and flourishes.

   Bibliography: p.
   1. Officers' wives--Handbooks, manuals, etc.
2. United States. Army--Military life--Handbooks,
manuals, etc. 3. Etiquette--United States--Handbooks,
manuals, etc. I. Title.
U766.B39 1988   355.1′336′0973   88-28476
ISBN 0-938936-79-4 (paper)
ISBN 0-938936-85-9 (cloth)

This book belongs to

_____

Contents

Special Thanks

Special thanks to five ladies whose encouragement and caring led to the writing of this book:

> Christy Burnes
>
> Marian Brandenburg
>
> Sheryl Stockwell
>
> Wanda Whisenhunt
>
> Barbara Curasi

Thanks also to:

> Sam Wilson
>
> Dave Stockwell*
>
> Danny Funk

Most of all, special thanks to my husband, Harry, for his love and support during the past twenty plus years and especially during the writing of this book.

*Author of *Tanks in the Wire*, Daring Books.

Introduction

There is much resource material available on etiquette, but very little on customs and courtesies of the military. Customs and courtesies should not complicate our lives, nor be a subject we worry about. Military customs are habits, procedures, traditions and even lore that has been passed down from generation to generation. Courtesies are traits of kindness, friendliness, thoughtfulness or consideration of others.

As the wife of a military officer for over twenty years, I have met many young wives who have expressed a genuine interest in learning these customs and courtesies of the military. It is primarily for these young women that *Ruffles & Flourishes* was developed and written.

I

Rank Insignia

Rank Insignia

The rank structure of the Army can be broken into three main categories: Enlisted Personnel, Warrant Officers and Commissioned Officers. The enlisted ranks are E1 through E9 with Noncommissioned Officer (NCO) ranks of E5 through E9. Warrant Officers have four steps—Warrant Officer 1 and Chief Warrant Officer 2, 3 and 4. A Warrant Officer is usually called, "Mister".

Within the Commissioned Officer ranks, there are also three categories. Company grade officers are: Second Lieutenant, First Lieutenant and Captain. Field grade officers are: Major, Lieutenant Colonel and Colonel. The general ranks are: Brigadier General, Major General, Lieutenant General and General.

ENLISTED RANK INSIGNIA AND PAYGRADES

 SERGEANT MAJOR OF THE ARMY (E-9)

 COMMAND SERGEANT MAJOR (E-9)

 SERGEANT MAJOR (E-9)

 FIRST SERGEANT (E-8)

 MASTER SERGEANT (E-8)

 SERGEANT FIRST CLASS (E-7)

 STAFF SERGEANT (E-6)

 SPECIALIST 6 (E-6)

 SERGEANT (E-5)

 SPECIALIST 5 (E-5)

 CORPORAL (E-4)

 SPECIALIST 4 (E-4)

 PRIVATE FIRST CLASS (E-3)

 PRIVATE (E-2)

E's are the paygrades.

WARRANT OFFICERS
RANK INSIGNIA
AND PAYGRADES

CHIEF
WARRANT
OFFICER (W4)

CHIEF
WARRANT
OFFICER (W3)

CHIEF
WARRANT
OFFICER (W2)

WARRANT
OFFICER (W1)

W's are the paygrades.

RUFFLES AND FLOURISHES

OFFICERS RANK INSIGNIA AND PAYGRADES

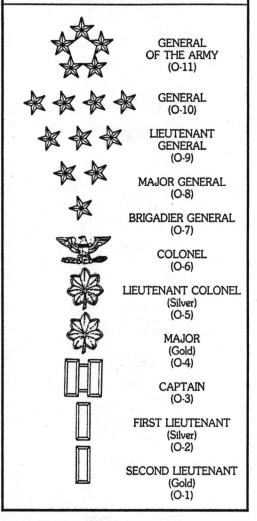

GENERAL OF THE ARMY (O-11)

GENERAL (O-10)

LIEUTENANT GENERAL (O-9)

MAJOR GENERAL (O-8)

BRIGADIER GENERAL (O-7)

COLONEL (O-6)

LIEUTENANT COLONEL (Silver) (O-5)

MAJOR (Gold) (O-4)

CAPTAIN (O-3)

FIRST LIEUTENANT (Silver) (O-2)

SECOND LIEUTENANT (Gold) (O-1)

O's are the paygrades.

18

II

Army
Structure

Army Structure

BRANCHES—If you look at your husband's uniform, you will see an insignia denoting his rank. You will also see another insignia—such as a tank over crossed sabers or crossed rifles. This insignia denotes his branch. All Commissioned Officers are members of a specific branch of the Army. These branches are organized into three categories: 1) Combat Arms, 2) Combat Support and 3) Combat Service Support. Each branch has a special color code which can be seen when the officer is wearing the "Army Blue Uniform" or "Army Blue Mess."

Combat Arms Branch

Armor (yellow)

Air Defense Artillery (scarlet)

Aviation (Ultramarine blue/golden orange)

Corps of Engineers (scarlet/white)

Field Artillery (scarlet)

Infantry (light blue)

Military Intelligence (blue)

Special Forces (forest green)

Combat Support Branch

Chemical Corps (cobalt blue/golden yellow)

Military Police Corps (green/white)

Signal Corps (orange/white)

Combat Service Support Branch

Advocate General's Corps (dark blue/scarlet)

Army Nurse Corps (maroon/white)

Chaplain Corps (black)

Dental Corps (maroon/white)

Finance Corps (silver gray/golden yellow)

Judge Advocate General's Corps (dark blue/white)

Medical Corps (maroon/white)

Medical Service Corps (maroon/white)

Ordinance (crimson/yellow)

Quartermaster (buff)

Transportation (brick red/golden yellow)

Veterinary Corps (maroon/white)

Note: The second color is used for piping.

The color for Warrant Officers is brown. Their color is branch immaterial because a Warrant Officer may be assigned to various branches.

UNITS

When you and your husband arrive at a new duty station, he will be assigned to a unit. He may work at the Platoon level, the Company level, or perhaps on the Brigade staff.

How large are these various units? How do they combine to become "the Army"? A brief description of the various units and their sizes will help you answer these questions:

The smallest combat unit is a **Crew**, Section, or Team consisting of four to six men and is led by a Noncommissioned Officer or a Lieutenant.

The next combat unit in size is a **Squad** (known as a Section in the Artillery and Aviation branches). It consists of about eight to eleven men and is led by a Sergeant or Staff Sergeant.

The next size is a **Platoon**, which consists of three or more Squads and is commanded by a Lieutenant (a Captain in Aviation units).

Three or more Platoons and their headquarters make up a **Company** (Troop or Battery), and is commanded by a Captain.

Two to four Companies (Troop or Battery) plus staff and headquarters make up a **Battalion** (or Squadron), and is commanded by a Lieutenant Colonel.

A **Brigade** (or Regiment) is made up of two to five Combat Battalions plus their headquarters, and is commanded by a Colonel. Separate Brigades may be commanded by a Brigadier General. A Regiment is similar in composition.

A **Division** is commanded by a Major General and is organized in different ways according to the type of Division. It usually consists of about 15,000 soldiers.

A **Corps** consists of two or more Divisions, their headquarters, and other organizations, and is commanded by a Lieutenant General.

Finally, a **Field Army** consists of two or more Army Corps, their headquarters and other organizations of all kinds.

Some noncombat or combat service units (medical, administrative) are organized differently to provide the best structure for their unit.

Okay, now you know where your husband works, but do you understand what he is saying when he talks about his job? The Army has a language all its own. The following list may help you wade through the sea of abbreviations and acronyms he may use:

Military Abbreviations and Acronyms

ACS:	Army Community Service
AER:	Army Emergency Relief
AG:	Adjutant General
AGI:	Annual General Inspection
AIT:	Advanced Individual Training
AR:	Army Regulations
ARCOM:	Army Commendation Medal
ARTEP:	Army Training Evaluation Program

Article 15:	Punishment other than Courts Martial imposed by the Company or Battalion Commander
ASAP:	As Soon As Possible
AVN:	Aviation
AWOL:	Absent without leave
Barracks:	Living quarters on post for single soldiers
Battalion Cdr:	Commanding Officer of the battalion, Lieutenant Colonel in rank
BDE:	Brigade
BDU:	Battle Dress Uniform
BN:	Battalion
BOQ:	Bachelor Officers' Quarters
Brigade Cdr:	Commanding Officer of the brigade, Colonel in rank
Cadre:	Permanently assigned personnel to a training or provisional unit or to a unit being newly organized
CDR:	Commander (previously abbreviated CO)
CG:	Commanding General
Commissary:	Military grocery store

Commissioned Officer:

A person commissioned by the United States Government through Congress and the President to be an officer in the armed forces of the United States

Company Cdr: Commanding Officer of the Company, Captain in rank

CONUS: Continental United States

CQ: Charge of Quarters

DA: Department of the Army

DB: Daily Bulletin

Detail: An assigned duty to one or more persons

DF: Distribution Form

DOD: Department of Defense

Duty Roster: Duty schedule maintained by unit First Sergeant

EER: Enlisted Efficiency Report

EM: Enlisted Man

Endorser: The person who endorses the enlisted/officer efficiency report

EOC: Emergency Operations Center

ETS: Expiration Term of Service

FM: Field Manual

FORSCOM: Forces Command

FTX:	Field Training Exercise
FY:	Fiscal Year
GED:	General Education Diploma—equivalent to a high school diploma
Grade:	Rank such as Sergeant, Private, Captain, etc.
HHC:	Headquarters & Headquarters Company
HOR:	Home of Record
IG:	Inspector General
JAG:	Judge Advocate General
JUMPS:	Joint Uniform Military Pay System
LOI:	Letter of Instruction
MilPerCen:	Military Personnel Center
MOS:	Military Occupational Specialty
MP:	Military Police
NA:	Not Applicable
NCO:	Noncommissioned Officer
NCOIC:	Noncommissioned Officer In Charge
NET:	Not Earlier Than
NG:	National Guard
NLT:	Not Later Than
OCS:	Officer Candidate School
OER:	Officer Evaluation Report
OIC:	Officer In Charge
OJT:	On the Job Training

Overseas duty:	A duty assignment outside the continental US, i.e. Korea, Germany, Alaska, Hawaii
OWC:	Officers' Wives Club
P-38:	A small can opener
PAO:	Public Affairs Office
PCS:	Permanent Change Of Station
Platoon Leader:	A Lieutenant in charge of a platoon
PLT:	Platoon
PMO:	Provost Marshal's Office
POV:	Privately Owned Vehicle
PX:	Post Exchange
Quarters:	Place of residence for military personnel and family members
RA:	Regular Army
Regimental CDR:	Commanding Officer of the Regiment, Colonel in rank
Regrets Only:	Call only if you cannot attend
ROTC:	Reserve Officer Training Corps
R & R:	Rest and Relaxation
RE-UP:	Reenlist
R.S.V.P.:	French, meaning, "Respondez s'il vous plait," or reply to the invitation as to whether or not you can attend
SDNCO:	Staff Duty Noncommissioned Officer

SDO:	Staff Duty Officer, officer in charge after working hours
Short Timer:	A soldier who has only minimum time left in the army
SOP:	Standard Operating Procedures
SQT:	Skill Qualification Test
Squadron Cdr:	Commanding Officer of the squadron, Lieutenant Colonel in rank
SSN:	Social security number
S-1:	Adjutant in charge of personnel
S-2:	In charge of intelligence and security
S-3:	In charge of training and operations
S-4:	In charge of logistics (supplies and equipment)
TDY:	Temporary duty
TOW:	An anti-tank missile system
TRADOC:	Training and Doctrine Command
Troop Cdr:	Commanding Officer of the troop, Captain in rank
USAR:	United States Army Reserves
WOC:	Warrant Officer Candidate
Warrant Officer:	An officer appointed by the Secretary of the Army to meet Army requirements for personnel with technical skills and knowledge
XO:	Executive Officer

Military Time

0100 hours = 1:00 AM
0200 hours = 2:00 AM
0300 hours = 3:00 AM
0400 hours = 4:00 AM
0500 hours = 5:00 AM
0600 hours = 6:00 AM
0700 hours = 7:00 AM
0800 hours = 8:00 AM
0900 hours = 9:00 AM
1000 hours = 10:00 AM
1100 hours = 11:00 AM
1200 hours = 12:00 Noon
1300 hours = 1:00 PM
1400 hours = 2:00 PM
1500 hours = 3:00 PM
1600 hours = 4:00 PM
1700 hours = 5:00 PM
1800 hours = 6:00 PM
1900 hours = 7:00 PM
2000 hours = 8:00 PM
2100 hours = 9:00 PM
2200 hours = 10:00 PM
2300 hours = 11:00 PM
2400 hours = 12 Midnight

The simplest way to figure civilian time for the afternoon and night time period is to subtract 1200 from the military time.

Examples:

      1600 hours − 1200 = 4:00 PM
      1330 hours − 1200 = 1:30 PM

III

Flags, Parades and Reviews

Flags, Parades and Reviews

One of the nice things about military life is attending the frequent parades and Change-Of-Command ceremonies. When we first arrived at Fort Knox, we went to either a parade or a Change-Of-Command ceremony almost every other week.

Parades, reviews, and Change-Of-Command ceremonies are considered official functions, so please try to attend. A formal invitation is extended for a review or Change-Of-Command, and it will require an R.S.V.P. Please remember to R.S.V.P., as customarily, seats are reserved by name for these occasions. Arrive about 15 minutes earlier than the time stated on the invitation. There is usually a seating chart and someone to show you to your seat.

"I remember one time my husband had made a reservation for me. When I arrived, an usher was there to seat me. I gave him my name and he said, 'Oh, yes, Mrs. Beam!' Then he walked up and down every single row looking at all the names. I said,

'I could have done that myself!' And he replied, 'Yes, ma'am.'"

Your attendance is important and please remember it is very important to R.S.V.P.

Regarding children, most of the time when you receive an invitation your children are allowed to attend, but they are probably not included in the reserved seating. If you desire to bring children to the ceremony, you must advise the hosting section how many children will attend. Otherwise, please arrange to have someone sit with them in the unreserved section. Once the ceremony begins, refrain from chatting and smoking. These are patriotic ceremonies and should be treated with respect.

Please Stand

These are times when you should stand:

Retreat—This is the daily ceremony of lowering the flag. This ceremony takes place outdoors at the flagpole. A detail of soldiers will be standing by the flagpole ready to lower and receive the flag. If you should be walking by the flagpole when the flag is being either raised or lowered, stop, face the flag, and render the appropriate honors. Maintain this position until the flag has been positioned or the music has stopped. If the retreat is sounded as you drive by, stop your car. You do not need to get out of the car, though you may if you choose. In any case, stop your car until the music finishes playing.

Ruffles & Flourishes—This is a song played when a General is present at an official event. It is only about eight notes and is played after "Attention" is sounded. It is played once for every star the senior General in attendance wears. Please stand when you hear the first note of Ruffles & Flourishes played.

The National Anthem and National Anthems of Foreign Countries—Please stand for our National Anthem. Salute the American flag by placing your hand over your heart during the playing of our National Anthem. If you are in a foreign country, you need to stand at the playing of their national anthem, but you do not salute their flag.

When Colors Pass in Review—This is usually performed at a parade, review or Change-Of-Command ceremony. The colors are carried by a dismounted (walking) unit. Stand when they are six paces before you, remain standing until they are six paces past, then you may sit. It is like a "wave" of people standing and then sitting as the colors pass by. As a note of interest, "colors" are flags carried by dismounted units and "standards" are flags carried by motorized units.

Service Songs—Army personnel and dependents should stand whenever the Army Song is played. A woman, out of courtesy, should also stand for all the service songs.

IV

Invitations
and
Replies

Invitations and Replies

Chances are you will receive and send many invitations during your spouse's military career. Socializing is an enjoyable part of military life. Please remember when entertaining, it does not have to be formal. It can also be casual.

The type of invitation received may determine the dress. The invitation should include these items: nature of occasion, day, date, hour, place and possibly the dress. Please be precise and brief when issuing an invitation.

Invitations are either formal or informal. They may be mailed, hand delivered, or issued by telephone. They should be sent out ten to fourteen days before the event and perhaps earlier for an event during the Christmas season.

Formal Invitations—may be engraved, semi-engraved, or handwritten, and they should be written in third person on light paper in black ink. You will receive formal invitations during your spouse's military career. They are usually for teas, luncheons, dinings in/out, reviews, formal dances or balls, or official receptions. They should be mailed two weeks in advance and answered within 24 hours of receipt. Completely engraved invitations are the most formal; however, the semi-engraved invitation is becoming more popular by those who entertain frequently. The commercial invitation allows the occasion and date to be written in and makes it convenient for use at large functions such as luncheons, unit parties, receptions, dinners and even parades and ceremonies.

See examples on pages 44 and 45.

Replies

Replies to formal invitations should be written in your best longhand on the front sheet of a folded, white, cream or off-white colored note paper. The reply should be the same as the invitation and be written in third person in black ink. Regrets would be written in the same way, but you may omit the time and place. You may include the reason for regretting, but it is not necessary.

Please remember to respond to a formal invitation within 24 hours, if possible, but no later than three days.

If the invitation is addressed to both husband and wife, then both of you should attend or neither of you should go alone. If your spouse is on duty, you should **not** attend alone.

When a telephone number is listed with an R.S.V.P., then a telephone reply is appropriate and should be answered within 24 hours, but not later than three days after you received the invitation.

See page 45.

Formal Invitations

Lieutenant Colonel and Mrs. Harry Smith

request the pleasure of the company of

Captain and Mrs. Jones

at dinner

on Saturday, the thirteenth of June

at eight o'clock

Quarters 1445 B

R.S.V.P.   *Black Tie*

Reply and Acceptance

Captain and Mrs. Michael Jones

accept with pleasure

the kind invitation of

Lieutenant Colonel and Mrs. Smith

to dinner

on Saturday, the thirteenth of June

at eight o'clock

Informal Invitations—These may be extended by telephone, personal note, note folded informal, message card, or calling card. Some hostesses prefer to telephone invitations, others like to write a personal note of invitation or use an informal card or calling card. Calling cards were encouraged years ago, but are not used quite as often these days. You may use them to extend an informal invitation. Your basic informal invitation should be on the outside of a fold-over note if it has no design and/or personalization, or on the inside if it does.

See examples, page 47.

Informal Invitations
(outside)

Dear Mrs. Brown,
   Will you and Captain Brown join us for dinner on Friday, May 17th at 8:00 P.M.?
      Sincerely,

         Betty Burns

(outside)

Colonel and Mrs. Robert Brown

(inside)

Cocktails
Friday, June 29th
6:00 - 8:00 pm
Regrets only

Flyers—A great way to get the word out to everyone! They should include all the necessary information with special details on how and where to R.S.V.P.

R.S.V.P. stands for "Respondez s'il vous plait" in French and translated means, "please reply". It may be written either R.S.V.P. or R.s.v.p. In any case, it must be answered.

I know, you are saying, "Oh no, not again!"...But R.S.V.P.ing really is a part of military life. As long as you associate with the military, you will receive invitations to which you should R.S.V.P. To be courteous, you need to respond within 24-48 hours. If there is a date on the R.S.V.P., you can wait until the deadline.

"Regrets Only" means just what it says. Call only if you cannot attend. You do not have to give a reason why you cannot attend.

There are some things which you should accept when you receive an invitation—New Year's Day Receptions, unit functions and post wide balls.

A **Thank You** to your hostess (within one or two days after the party) is a MUST. This may be expressed by telephone, in person, or by a thank you note. The envelope and note should be addressed to the hostess only.

V

Social Functions

Social Functions

One of the nicest traditions in the military is the social life. We are given an opportunity to meet and associate with a variety of people and are able to build lasting relationships from these social exchanges. Listed below are a variety of social functions:

Coffees are probably the most popular social functions because they are warm, casual, inexpensive, and a nice way to entertain a large group. Unit coffees are also popular. These days, unit coffees are held more often in the evening because of the number of women who work. Not everyone drinks coffee, so it is advisable to offer another beverage such as tea or punch. The refreshments should be simple and may even be purchased at a bakery. Dress is usually casual—many times when you receive an invitation to a coffee it will list the dress.

Teas are a little bit more formal than coffees and are usually held in the mid-afternoon. Teas should be planned in advance, and should have a friendly and relaxed atmosphere. They should never be so formal that people feel uncomfortable attending. Little sandwiches, cookies, tarts, nuts, candies or mints may be served. The food served should be small enough to handle easily while holding a cup and saucer.

Please remember if you use candles, they should be lit. Candles should not be used as decorations. If you use them, light them.

Dress for a tea is a church dress or nice suit.

Asked to pour? It is an honor to be asked to pour at a tea and one should thank the hostess for the honor. Ladies who are to pour will probably be asked a day or two in advance and be given an appropriate time to arrive. Each person is asked to pour for 15 to 20 minutes.

Coffee outranks tea, a custom that grew because most American women prefer coffee to tea. Because of this custom, the honored guest or most senior guest would have the honor of pouring coffee. The next most senior lady, tea, etc. At a large function when coffee and tea are served together, these beverages outrank punch. In other words, the wife of the highest ranking officer should be asked to pour the coffee, then the second highest to pour the tea or punch. If all three beverages are served, the wife of the third highest ranking officer should pour the punch.

Since the senior wives are asked to pour at official teas, it would be nice to ask the junior wives to pour at smaller functions. Start with the most junior wife and work upward. This could be a great opportunity to help them become involved.

> *"When we were in Germany and my husband was a Company Commander, our Battalion Commander's wife was having a tea for the new Brigade Commander's wife. She decided that all the Company Commanders' wives would pour, but she found out I was left-handed and I was not allowed to pour. If you notice, most punch ladles are designed for a right-handed person. Thank goodness times have changed!"*

Farewells/Welcomes
for Commanders' Wives

Often a function is planned to farewell or welcome the wife of a commander of a battalion/squadron, brigade/regiment or a post. When the lady being farewelled or welcomed is the wife of the Commanding General of a post, then the officers' wives club and the senior officers' wives group normally do the planning. The executive officers' wives usually organize the function for the wife of a Brigade or Battalion Commander. The function is usually a tea, coffee, luncheon or dinner.

It is not a good idea to plan one function to jointly welcome and farewell the incoming and outgoing ladies. The incoming lady should be welcomed within one week of her arrival but never later than two weeks.

Whether planning a farewell or welcome, the guidelines are basically the same. About 8 to 10 weeks prior to the change of command, organize a meeting to discuss ideas for the farewell and welcome. Ladies invited to this meeting may include:

A. At Brigade level; wives of Battalion commanders, wives of Brigade staff and the wife of the Brigade CSM (Command Sergeant Major)

B. At Battalion level; wives of Company Commanders, wives of Battalion staff, wife of Battalion CSM, and wives of Company First Sergeants.

Before the meeting, have an agenda ready.

Always check with the outgoing first lady for a date most convenient for her.

Organize and delegate people to help with the following committees: 1. Invitations 2. Reservations 3. Name tags 4. Menu 5. Pouring 6. Decorations 7. Escorts 8. Receiving Line 9. Funds. Some committees can be combined, such as invitations and name tags, or reservations and pouring.

Planning a farewell/welcome for a Commander's wife requires a lot of preparation. Please remember that common sense is very important. It is also necessary to communicate often with both ladies and ask their advice, after all, they are the ladies being honored.

Invitations

Formal invitations should be sent, if possible. They should be handwritten or engraved, in the third person in black ink. The appropriate invitation for a farewell/welcome is not a foldover card, but a single card, 5 3/8″ wide by 4 1/4″ high. See example, page 59. The handwriting for invitations and envelopes should be the same. Invitations should be sent two to three weeks before the function. Write a separate note asking ladies to pour and fasten the note to the invitation.

Name Tags

Name tags should be written before the function. Use Mrs. Smith for wives of General Officers and wives of full Colonels. Write Mrs. John Smith, not Mrs. Mary Smith, on other name tags.

Receiving Line

There are several ways to form the receiving line, so choose and use the best way for your particular needs:

1. Use the wife of the Brigade or Battalion Executive Officer as the adjutant (announcer).

2. Use the wife of the senior Battalion or Company Commander as the adjutant.

3. If welcoming the wife of a Brigade Commander, use the wife of each Battalion Commander to serve as adjutant for the ladies in her Battalion. This would help the incoming wife associate new faces with particular Battalions.

4. Use the S1 of the Brigade or Battalion as the adjutant (the S1 may be a female).

The receiving line would consist of the adjutant (announcer), the wife of the Brigade or Battalion Executive Officer, and the wife of the outgoing or incoming Commander.

Escorts

When possible, planning should include providing an escort for the guest of honor from and back to her quarters.

In addition to the guest of honor, other senior ladies should be provided with an escort/hostess at the function. The escort would greet her lady, help with her coat, find her name tag, accompany her through the receiving line and see that she is warmly welcomed.

Pouring

As stated previously, it is an honor to be asked to pour. In most circumstances, pouring should be done according to the husband's rank and also according to the beverage. Normally, the guest of honor does not pour.

The pouring committee should compile a list of ladies who will pour in order of their husbands' date of rank, listing the time they will pour and what beverage. At a farewell/welcome function, the pouring time for each lady should be approximately ten minutes. If a pourer is late, just continue down the list.

A few suggestions as to who you would ask to pour: at the Brigade level, the wives of the Command Group, plus wives of Battalion Commanders and staff; at Battalion level, the wives of the staff and Company Commanders.

Farewell/Welcome Invitation

(For Brigade Commander's wife)

The Ladies of the Second Brigade

United States Army Armor Center

request the pleasure of your company

at a

Luncheon

In honor of

Mrs. David Brown

on Tuesday, the ninth of June

at

eleven thirty o'clock

Fort Knox Officers Club

R.S.V.P.

942-6645

by the sixth of June

Brunches

This is a favorite because there is so much food. Brunch is usually a combination of breakfast and lunch. It is normally served closer to lunchtime, but with breakfast food. Remember the most important rule for a brunch is: serve as soon as the guests arrive. The attire is usually a dress, simple suit, a skirt and blouse or sweater, or dressy slacks. It is a nice affair and a very special way to welcome or farewell someone.

Luncheons

A luncheon is a pleasant way for a wife to entertain. She can keep the luncheon simple and informal or become very formal and precise. If the luncheon is informal, attractive matching paper placemats, plates, cups and napkins may even be used. Often, luncheons are given by a unit or wives' club. Almost every Army post has an Officers' Wives Club which has a monthly luncheon. This is a great way to meet people. A social "sherry" hour is usually planned prior to the luncheon. Reservations are a *MUST*. It is important to make a reservation, keep it, or cancel by the deadline to avoid being charged for it. Many OWC luncheons have informative programs. The attire is usually a dress or skirt and blouse. Dressy slacks and a blouse may be appropriate, depending on the formality of your particular post.

Cocktail Parties

These are essentially stand up affairs and usually held for a two hour period. The invitation will state from 5 to 7, or 6 to 8 PM. If the invitation states from 5 to 7, you do not need to arrive at 5 o'clock, but you **do** need to leave by 7 o'clock. The food served will be light, such as finger foods, chips and dips, or cheese. The invitation should specify the dress.

Cocktail Buffets

Basically, these are the same as the cocktail party, but with substantial food. Many times they are for a longer period of time than cocktail parties. Food is served buffet style and you may eat standing, since chairs may not be available for everyone to sit.

Buffet Suppers

This is the most popular way to serve dinner to guests. Unlike the cocktail buffet, liquor is not always served at buffet suppers. The food is prepared by the hostess and is served buffet style, so you may have to eat standing up. This is sometimes done on purpose to encourage guests to mingle and to get to know one another.

Dinner

There may be times when you will want to be a bit more formal and arrange a seated dinner for your guests. Please remember you will be limited to the number of guests you may invite and it will entail more work than a cocktail buffet or buffet supper. You are the hostess, cook and server. It is a nice way to entertain because everyone can sit down and not have to worry about balancing a plate on their laps. Please remember that a sit-down dinner does not have to be formal. It can be casual. See examples of table settings, pages 64-66.

Bridal & Baby Showers

Traditionally, a shower is given for a bride to be or an expectant mother and is almost always given by a close friend. Since gifts are involved, it is very important that the guest list be made up of friends and not merely acquaintances. A shower is proper for first babies, but there is no rule against them for later arrivals, so please use your own judgment. Sometimes showers are given by a unit, so if you have recently arrived on a post and are new to the unit, you may not know the honoree. This unit will be your family for the next few years and it remains your choice whether or not you want to attend.

Potlucks

These are becoming popular as large group functions. It is because no one person has to do all the work and all invited guests contribute to the meal. We usually had a potluck every month in our squadron at Fort Knox, and it was really nice. Everyone brings a dish and the variety of food is great.

Unit Parties

The structure of units was discussed in Chapter 2. Most units will hold some type of "Hail & Farewell" either at battalion/squadron or company/troop level. A "Hail & Farewell" is a function planned to welcome new people and farewell those who are leaving the unit. This is an excellent way to build camaraderie and unity, but depends on everyone's support and participation to be successful.

Please remember that people don't entertain to torture you or themselves. It is done for enjoyment, so relax and have fun. No one has ever been harmed by "social ineptitude." Most of the time, no one even notices if you've made an error. Please be yourself, and the rest will come easily!

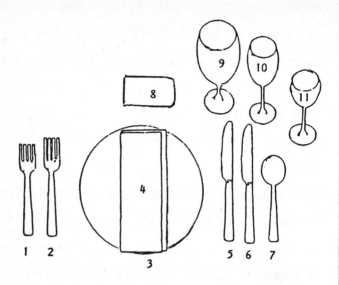

Formal Table Setting

For all table settings the silverware is used starting with the farthest from the plate first!

1 salad fork   7 soup spoon

2 meat fork   8 name card

3 plate   9 water glass

4 napkin   10 wine glass

5 meat knife   11 champagne glass

6 salad knife

Note: for a very formal table fresh forks and knives would be used and extra wine glasses brought out with the courses they accompany.

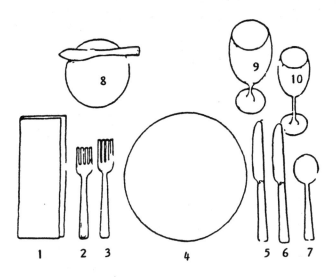

Informal Table Setting

1 napkin

2 salad fork

3 meat fork

4 plate

5 meat knife

6 salad knife

7 soup spoon

8 bread and butter plate

9 water glass

10 wine glass

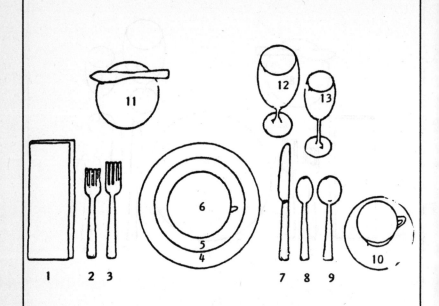

Basic Table Setting

1 napkin

2 salad fork

3 dinner fork

4 dinner plate

5 salad plate

6 soup cup

7 dinner knife

8 coffee spoon

9 soup spoon

10 coffee cup & saucer

11 bread & butter plate

12 water glass

13 wine glass

VI

Receptions, Receiving Lines, Dining In/ Dining Out

Receptions, Receiving Lines Dining In/ Dining Out

Receptions—Receiving Lines

Receptions are usually planned to honor special guests. They may be formal or informal, large or small. For instance, receptions are held at Fort Knox to honor the Armor Officer Basic and Armor Officer Advance Course students and wives. Receptions may also be held for special events such as: weddings, anniversaries, changes of command ceremonies or New Year's Day.

Whatever the type of reception, the rules of etiquette are the same. Not all receptions have receiving lines, but they are common in the military. The receiving line consists of the host, hostess and the honorees. The reception line consists of the guests being received.

Receiving Line

It is usually formed from right to left, although this may not always be practical. From "right to left" means an officer stands to the right of the spouse. The order of the receiving line could be aide or adjutant, host, hostess, guest of honor, guest of honor's wife, and then other honorees according to rank. It is not advisable to have a woman at the end of the line. See example, page 76.

The function of the aide is not to receive but to give the guests' names to the host. Do not shake his/her hand.

A woman's club receiving line has the president first, next, the guests of honor, followed by others who may have been invited to be in the line.

If you are in the receiving line, arrive at least ten minutes before the time scheduled for the reception to begin so you will be in place at the time announced.

Reception Line

Please arrive a few minutes early in order to check your wrap and locate your place in the line. The officer will step up to the aide and introduce first the spouse and then him/herself. Remember, ladies precede their escorts through the receiving line.

"I remember this because when we first arrived at Fort Knox, at one of our first receptions, the men started through first. The senior officer, Colonel Clark, was the first in line and said, 'Oh, my goodness, don't hide that lovely lady behind you!' So all the ladies preceded their husbands. I always remember this because he said it in such a nice way. The only time the ladies don't go first is in the Air Force or at the White House."

Keep it brief. This is no time for a long discussion. If your name is said incorrectly, it is proper to correct it. Don't carry a drink or cigarette when going through the line.

Gloves

There was a time when gloves were worn in receiving lines. When we first came to Fort Knox in 1968, I went out and bought beige, black, and white gloves with shoes and purses to match. Customs have changed, but I really think with all sincerity that we will return to wearing gloves. The rule of thumb is, if the people in the receiving line have on gloves, then you wear gloves. When you arrive at a post, you can call the protocol officer or adjutant of your unit to find out whether or not you will need to wear gloves.

"I remember one New Year's Day Reception when we should have worn gloves. Fortunately, two of the girls brought gloves with them, so we'd take them off and pass them down the line behind us. In this way four of us each had one glove! It is a little tricky wearing the left glove on your right hand. And it's certainly more comfortable to wear both gloves!"

If you do wear gloves, remember to remove them if you smoke, eat or drink. Put them in your purse or somewhere out of sight, do not just hold them in your hands.

Dining-In/Dining-Out

A Dining-In is a formal occasion arranged by a unit or organization in order to boost morale. Traditionally, it was a stag affair for male officers only, but now it is fashionable to invite spouses. It is then called a Dining-Out.

The term, "Dining-In", is derived from an old Viking tradition of celebrating battles by a formal ceremony. A Dining-In or Dining-Out involves much more than just a dinner. It may also include a receiving line, cocktail hour, posting and retirement of the colors ceremony, punch ceremony, toasts, etc.

The **dress** is formal for either a Dining-In or Dining-Out, which means a long or short formal gown or formal tea length dress for ladies, and for men: Army blue or white uniform with bow tie or Army blue or white mess.

There are two officers of the mess: the President, who is usually the Commanding Officer, and the Vice, called, "Mr. Vice".

The President sets the date and place of the Dining-In, arranges for the guest speaker and invites the Chaplain to give the Invocation. He also appoints other mess officers to serve as committee chairmen (example: table arrangements, dining room arrangements, such as menu and public address system, and protocol committee). The President also introduces the guest speaker and other honored guests. He appoints Mr. Vice.

Mr. Vice is usually a junior officer selected for his wit. He is the first to arrive and the last to leave. He starts the cocktail period by opening the lounge, sounds the dinner chime when dinner is ready, delivers the appropriate toasts and keeps the party moving.

Invitations should be mailed two weeks to a month before the date set for the dinner. A formal invitation is appropriate, they may be handwritten, printed or the fill-in type. Invitations must state the type of uniform to be worn.

The menu usually consists of four or five courses and is traditionally beef (roast or steak).

Seating—At a Dining-In, the guest of honor sits to the right of the President at the head table, with the next ranking guest on the President's left. Other guests are then seated throughout the room. The members of the mess are seated according to seniority, with Mr. Vice at the foot of the table.

At a Dining-Out, the guest of honor's wife is seated to the right of the President and the President's wife is seated to the right of the guest of honor. See example, page 77.

Toasting

Toasts are made to people and occasions. The following is an example:

    "I propose a toast to...

        ...the United States of America."

        Response: "To the United States!"

...the President of the United States."
Response: "To the President!"

...the President of the Republic of Botswana."
Response: "To the President!"

Note: Toasts would be made for the countries present at the Dining-In/Dining-Out.

...to the United States Army."
Response: "To the Army!"

Note: Toasts would be made to the different services present.

The rule is usually one sip to a toast. The person to whom the toast is being made does not toast, to do so would be to toast one's self. You do not need to drink alcohol; however, do not put your glass upside down or hold your hand over the wine glass to avoid receiving alcohol, simply raise the glass to your lips, but do not drink if you do not wish to consume alcohol.

Example - Receiving Line

FLAG LINE

| 1 | 2 | 3 | 4 |

A   B   C   D   E   F

Carpet

A - Adjutant or Aide

B - Host

C - Hostess

D - Honored Guest (Officer)

E - Honored Guest (Spouse)

F - Any Gentleman

1 - U.S. National Flag

2 - Foreign National Flags (alphabetically)

3 - Organizational Flags

4 - Generals' or Admirals' Flags

Example - Dining Out

FLAG STAND

. . . .

D   B   A   C   E

X   X   X   X   X   X   X   X

A - President

B - Guest Speaker

C - Guest Speaker's Wife

D - President's Wife

E - Chaplain

Mr. Vice

VII

Dress

Dress

Dress is determined by local customs, the post protocol, what looks good on you, and what you can afford. It also depends on the type of invitation received and the time of day of the function. As a rule of thumb, the later in the day it is, the dressier the dress. "What to wear?" is an often asked question. We are always concerned about wearing what is proper, when in reality, most women dress properly. When in doubt about what to wear, a skirt and blouse is always acceptable. The important issue is to feel comfortable and at ease when attending social functions.

There are four classifications of dress:

Formal

    Ladies—Long or short formal dress
              Tea length formal (mid calf)
              Fancy cocktail dress

Men—Army blue uniform with bow tie

Army white uniform with bow tie

Army blue mess or white mess shown as "black tie"
on invitation

Tuxedo

Informal

Ladies—Cocktail dress

Long skirt

Evening pants ensemble

Church dress

Fancy skirt and blouse (depends on type
of function)

Men—Army blue or white uniform w/four-in-hand tie

Army green uniform

Business suit or sports jacket with tie

Casual

Ladies—Simple dress

Skirt and blouse

Dressy slacks (pants) with blouse

Men—Sport coat and slacks with or without a tie

Very Casual

Ladies—Slacks

Jeans

Shorts

Men—Slacks

Jeans

Shorts

Once, I received an invitation to a pool party and I **knew** what to wear. That is where **common sense** comes in. Remember, if you are in doubt about what to wear and it is not on the invitation, call the hostess. At other times the adjutant of your unit will know. He should be aware of what the appropriate dress is for a function if it was planned by the unit.

VIII

If You Please

If You Please

Courtesy is kindness and consideration towards people we come in contact with. A lot of courtesies are second nature because they were taught to us by our parents, teachers, etc. The following are simply good behavior:

Promptness

When my husband first came into the military, we were invited to the Colonel's home. Because we were so concerned about not being late, we showed up 15 minutes early and the Colonel was putting on his shoes! At the next post, we decided we would not be so early this time and we were 15 minutes late. Well, it was our welcome and we missed it! Needless to say, the next place we were on time. It is good to be as close to the time listed as possible, just one or two minutes either way. And please be at ease. You have been invited because you are important to the unit, so enjoy yourself.

Friendliness

Don't be afraid to approach people you don't know and introduce yourself. When I was younger, I was so shy that I was really pleased when someone would come up to me and talk. I didn't have the nerve to approach someone else. I'm sure there are other people like that.

Consideration

Introduce yourself to senior officers, NCO's, their ladies, and guests of honor at functions. This is your responsibility. It is not apple polishing! When we go to receptions, I try to talk with as many people as I can, but sometimes I just don't have enough time. If you come up to me, then I feel better about leaving, knowing I have met many new people.

Politeness

Thank the host and hostess when you leave their party. Sometimes it is easier to just leave, but please resist the temptation and thank the host or hostess for the invitation.

Thoughtfulness

Don't feel you must stay until the senior person leaves. Many of you will be paying for babysitting, so it is understandable if you have to leave early for that or another important reason. When my husband was Professor of Military Science at

Marshall University, a Dining-Out was arranged at Christmas for all the ROTC cadets. It was a formal occasion and the Sergeant Major put out the word that no one could leave until the Colonel left. We were having a good time, and were not ready to leave at an early hour. However, realizing that some people needed to leave, we walked out the door and around the block. Several couples left and then we were able to come back in and continue having a good time. If you do have to leave early, please remember to say goodbye to the senior person before you leave. Afterwards, write or phone your thanks to the hostess.

Respect

Be yourself. If you are invited to a formal dinner, you do not need to return it with a formal dinner. If what you enjoy the most is cooking hamburgers, that's great! Just be casual and as informal as you want. Most of all, do it because you want to and not because you feel it is expected.

Kindness

Write or phone your thanks after a party. The hostess put a lot of time and effort into planning and preparing for the party, so a simple thank you from a guest means a lot.

IX

Potpourri

Potpourri

Calling Cards

In the past, calling cards were a necessity, but today they are seldom used. Here are some hints on what you can do with calling cards if you have them:

- send them with flowers or gifts
- as informal party invitations
- as reminders
- as bearers of messages of condolence or congratulations
- as acceptances or regrets to informal events

Courtesy Call on the Commander

Years ago when you arrived on a post, you arranged for a visit with the Brigade or Regimental Commander. The size and complexity of today's Army hinders this custom. Most places now have replaced this tradition with the New Year's Day Reception. When you arrive on post, check with your unit adjutant and he will know the unit and/or post policy.

Chaplains and Physicians

Chaplains are addressed as Chaplain Jones or Father Smith. Physicians and dentists are addressed by their military rank; however, you may address them as, Doctor, when a patient in the clinic.

Suzy Smith or Mrs. Smith?

It's "Mrs. Smith" unless she says, "Call me, Suzy." And if she says, "Call me, Suzy," she really means it. So relax and call her, Suzy. It's perfectly fine.

Alcohol

Alcohol is served at most functions, but you do not need to drink. Remember this is a personal matter.

> *"When we first came in the Army, we were at a party and a colonel insulted me for drinking a Shirley Temple. He said I was being unsociable because I was not drinking alcohol! It did happen!"*

Parties don't mean you have to drink alcohol. **IT IS YOUR CHOICE!**

Gum

Do not chew gum at official functions, church, cocktail parties, or other social gatherings. It is not lady-like, or dignified.

X

Questions

Questions

1. Does a wife wear her husband's rank?

There is no rank among women, however, she does have a position created by her husband's rank. She should never forget that it is his position and his rank. When speaking of him, she refers to him as Dave or Bob, never as, "the Major" or, "the Colonel". When you want to be formal, say, "my husband".

2. How is a female officer addressed?

When addressing a female officer under circumstances when the use of, "sir" would be appropriate for a male officer, the term, "ma'am" should be used.

3. How do you address Noncommissioned Officers?

Noncommissioned Officers are addressed by their titles. Sergeants Major are addressed as, "Sergeant Major". All other

Sergeants are referred to simply as, "Sergeant". A Specialist is addressed as, "Specialist". Privates and recruits need only be addressed by their last names.

4. When is it proper to smoke at a social function?

If no ashtrays are displayed, you do not smoke. If you are a guest in someone's home, you also do not smoke during the meal.

5. Is it okay to decline an invitation to a social function and then accept if we can attend?

NO. Once you decline an invitation, you cannot accept unless you are invited a second time.

6. What is the proper way to make an introduction?

Introduce younger to older, man to woman, one person to a group; the name given first is the person to whom deference is being shown. Example: "Mrs. Smith, may I present Major Edwards?"

7. How should an invitation be addressed, Mrs. Jane Smith or Mrs. John Smith?

Mrs. John Smith. Mrs. Jane Smith is used only if she is divorced.

8. Should I R.S.V.P. if the invitation doesn't call for it?

Yes, a thoughtful guest will let her hostess know if she can attend.

9. When at a large dinner held at a restaurant or the club, who starts to eat first?

The hostess, who is usually the wife of the senior man of the group sponsoring the affair.

10. What is the proper procedure to follow with a napkin?

It is unfolded and placed on your lap. A small napkin should be fully unfolded and a large napkin left folded in half. After the meal, place the napkin beside your plate.

11. What is the proper word used in reference to U.S. military installations for the various services?

An Army installation is a Post; a Navy and Air Force installation is a Base; a Marine Corps installation is a Camp.

Reflections

Reflections

Strive for self-development. In the military, your husband will be provided opportunities for growth in his professional development—encourage him and be interested in what he accomplishes. The Army will send him to school throughout his career. Your long-range plans and goals should include growing with him. Go to school. Take craft classes. Participate in unit and community activities. How you grow is up to you.

In essence, your husband's duties and responsibilities will change as he progresses in rank. Expand your horizons and enjoy the changes. Above all, "be yourself." If you take these attitudes of growth and help each other, you will become each other's best friend. Your husband will have confidence in you and trust you to support him, and your time in the military will be rewarding.

The Army truly can be a pleasant and unique way of life. I've enjoyed the last twenty plus years, except for a few moments here and there. Wherever you go, there is something nice about every post. Always be positive and, wherever you are, leave a little bit of sunshine and bloom where you are planted!

Bibliography

A Guide to Protocol & Etiquette for Official Entertainment,
Headquarters, DA Pamphlet 600-60, April 1981.

Customs & Courtesies of the Service, FC 7-161, August 1984.

Aviation Officers Wives' Guide, Fort Rucker, 1984.

The Officers Family Social Guide, by Mary Preston Gross,
Library of Congress Catalog Card #77-72724.

The Once Over Lightly, by Bibs Reynard.

A Leading Lady, by Silja Allen.

Service Etiquette, by Oretha D. Swartz, Third Edition, 1985.

1st Class Customs and Courtesies in the Military, 1st Infantry Division and Ft. Riley, KS, December 1984.

The Army Officers Guide, by LTC Lawrence P. Crocker, U.S.
Army (Ret.), Stackpole Books.